THE LAWYER'S BIG BOOK OF FUN

Arnold Kanter and Jodi Kanter • Illustrated by Tony Tallarico

CONTEMPORARY
BOOKS
A TRIBUNE NEW MEDIA COMPANY

Library of Congress Cataloging-in-Publication Data

Kanter, Arnold B., 1942–
    The lawyer's big book of fun / Arnold B. Kanter, Jodi I. Kanter,
and Tony Tallarico.
        p.   cm.
    ISBN 0-8092-3410-6
    1. Lawyers—Humor.   I. Kanter, Jodi I.   III. Tallarico, Tony.
III. Title.
PN6231.L4K36   1995
818'5402—dc20   95-37170
                                          CIP

Other legal books by Arnold Kanter:
The Secret Memoranda of Stanley J. Fairweather
The Handbook of Law Firm Mismanagement
Advanced Law Firm Mismanagement
The Ins & Outs of Law Firm Mismanagement

Interior design by Hespenheide Design

Published by Contemporary Books, Inc.
Two Prudential Plaza, Chicago, Illinois 60601-6790
Manufactured in the United States of America
International Standard Book Number: 0-8092-3410-6
10   9   8   7   6   5   4   3   2   1

CONTENTS

INTRODUCTION

Being a lawyer isn't all that much fun, is it? OK, sometimes it is. But not usually. What would you say—maybe 28 percent of the time? Less? . . . Oh, we're sorry.

Why isn't being a lawyer fun? That's the question. Here are the six prime reasons, as determined by a highly scientific study:

1. ungrateful clients
2. disreputable opposing attorneys
3. imperious judges
4. disloyal partners
5. overdemanding young associates
6. no *Lawyer's Big Book of Fun*

We can't do a darn thing about the first five. And, let's face it, neither can you. But—look what we've got here—is it—? Yes, we think it is! Well, son-of-a-gun. . . . A *Lawyer's Big Book of Fun*.

Will this funbook make you ecstatic? Content in your practice and personal life? C'mon now, for a few bucks you want what thousands of dollars and years of therapy won't get you, either? Be realistic. Would you settle for a chuckle or two, a momentary uptick in your disposition? Good. We've got a deal; let's go.

HOW THIS BOOK IS ORGANIZED

Randomly.

Look, we know you're a lawyer. We know you expect a chapter on how the book is organized, a chapter on how to use the book, an index, a bibliography, and several hundred footnotes. But hey, c'mon, this is a *funbook*. Lighten up a little. . . .

There, that's better.

CONFIDENCE BUILDERS

Law is a tough business—we know. Every smart person who can't stand the sight of blood goes to law school these days (except the excessively greedy types, who wind up in business school). That means the competition is fierce. And then there are those demanding clients who make a big fuss over every little million-dollar mistake.

So in a profession like law, you need your confidence boosted once in a while. When you feel that need, turn to one of the Confidence Builders in this book, marked thusly:

If you have trouble with these Confidence Builders, watch for our next book, *The Lawyer's Remedial Big Book of Fun*.

FIND THE BEAR

Some of your litigation partners are camping over the weekend to plan their marketing strategy for next year. What they don't know is that there's a great big bear in the woods waiting to eat them up. If you can find the bear, you might be able to save them! (On the other hand, if they're such tough litigators, maybe you should let them save themselves.)

3

LAWYER DRESS-UP

If you look lawyerly, it doesn't matter how much law you know. You'll get ahead.
Dress up Lawyer Larry and Attorney Annie. (No cross-dressing, please; this is a
respectable funbook.)

L.L. COOL-CAP

L.L. MOST IMPORTANT PAPERS

A.A. NOTEBOOK COMPUTER

L.L. JEANS

L.L. OR A.A. WALL STREET JOURNAL

L.L. JOGGING PANTS

L.L. OR A.A. CARRY AROUND

EMERGENCY PACIFIER LL· OR A·A·

L.L. OR A.A. BIKE HELMET

A·A· OR L·L· BASEBALL CAP, MUST BE WORN BACKWARD.

L.L. DRESS, PARTY AND OFFICE SUIT

A.A. DRESS, PARTY AND OFFICE WEAR

A.A. MINISKIRT

A.A. WEIGHT-LOSS JOGGING OUTFIT

ANYTIME BAUBLE A.A.

L.L. JOGGING JACKET

L.L. COUNTRY-WESTERN SHIRT

A.A. OR L.L. ANYTIME CAP

OVERSIZED TURTLENECK A.A. OR L.L.

GETTING FROM A TO Z

Alice Baker-Carr is a member of the Alphabetical Bar Committee. She is on a very important mission. She must find all the letters of the alphabet, from *A* to *Z*, hidden throughout this city. Maybe you can help Alice. She certainly could use it.

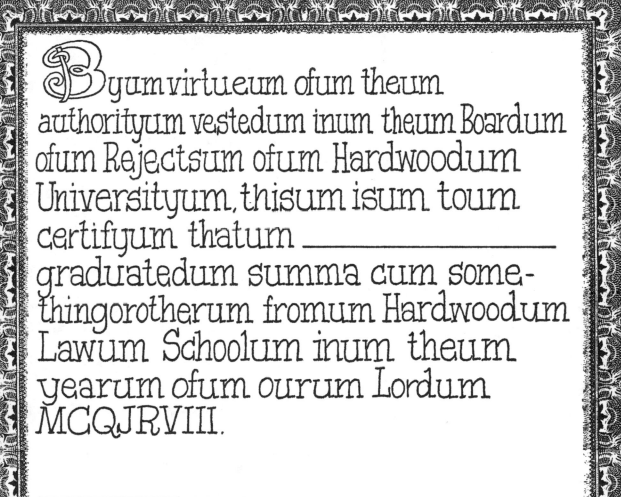

By um virtueum ofum theum authorityum vestedum inum theum Boardum ofum Rejectsum ofum Hardwoodum Universityum, thisum isum toum certifyum thatum _____ graduatedum summa cum some-thingorotherum fromum Hardwoodum Lawum Schoolum inum theum yearum ofum ourum Lordum MCQJRVIII.

_____
President, Hardwood University

_____
Good Friend, President of Hardwood U.

COLOR BORDER "GREEN" – USE DOLLAR BILL FOR REFERENCE. WHEN COMPLETED, SEND REFERENCE TO US.

MATCH LATIN TO ENGLISH

A really good lawyer ought to be able to fake at least a little Latin.
Match the phrase in the left column with the correct meaning in the right column.

1. de novo

2. Bie Mir Bist Du Schön.

3. mens rea

4. reductio ad absurdum

5. zuppa di potate parmigiana

6. illegitimata non carborundum

7. non compos mentis

8. It speaks for itself.

a. You gotta be kidding.

b. playing with somewhat less than a full deck

c. from de beginning

d. Don't let the bastards grind you down.

e. res ipsa loquitur

f. You're very nice-looking.

g. opposite of women's rea

h. potato soup with Parmesan cheese

[Answers: 1. c; 2. f; 3. g; 4. a; 5. h; 6. d; 7. b; 8. e]

8

AVOID THE PIT

The lawyer's road to success is loaded with all sorts of hazards.
Can you help Indiana Tomes avoid the pitfalls?

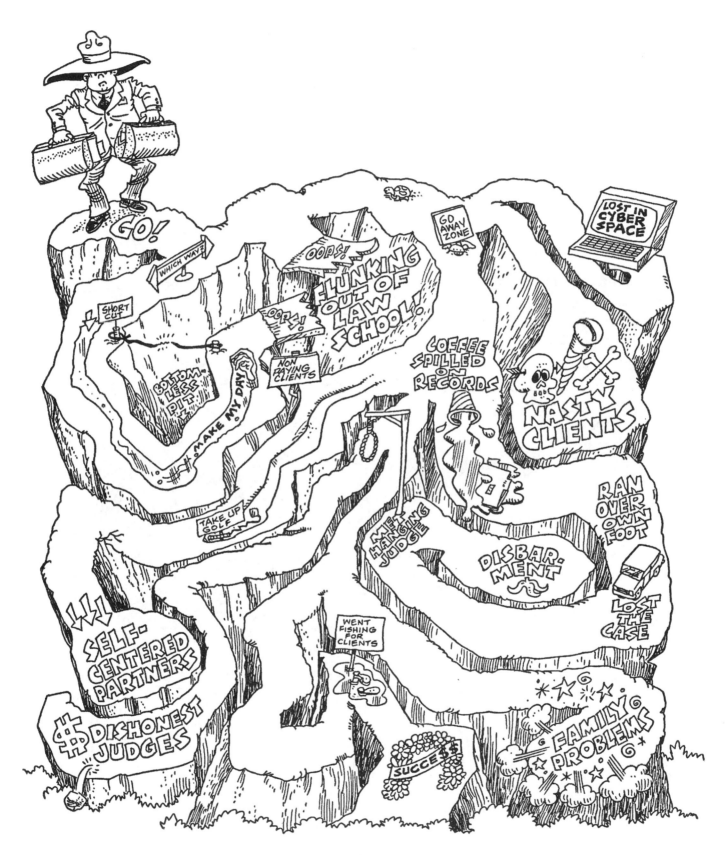

THE LUNCHEON BILL

You have invited your client, Tammy Goldhurst, out to lunch at a restaurant you've never been to before. The restaurant turns out to be a lot more expensive than you thought. You ordered a house salad ($4.25), lobster ($29.50), and pecan pie à la mode ($5.75). You also had two drinks, at $3.50 each. Tammy, who is on a diet, ordered consommé ($2.25), the dieter's delight ($6.75), and no dessert. She had coffee, which was $1.50. What is your share of the bill?

[Answer: "Why don't we just split it?"]

WHICH THINGS GO WITH THE LAWYER?

Some of these items are associated with lawyers and some with other kinds of
professionals. See if you can pick out the lawyer's things from the rest.

THE ALPHABET GAME

Remember those long car trips when you were a kid? Remember how Mom and Dad kept you busy finding all the letters of the alphabet—in order—on street signs? And how when you got to Z they'd bet you couldn't do it again and you would? And how after you did it again they'd bet you couldn't find ten *Q*s in less than an hour and you did but it took you an hour and a half? You gave them a pretty easy time of it back then, didn't you?

Well, now there's the Alphabet Game for Lawyers! Keep your kids and colleagues busy finding the letters of these legal words and phrases on the road:

❏ JURISDICTION   ❏ HERE COME DA JUDGE

❏ QUID PRO QUO   ❏ INTENTIONAL TORT

❏ EXCULPATORY   ❏ INVOLUNTARY MANSLAUGHTER

❏ RES IPSA LOQUITUR   ❏ DECLARATION OF CONDOMINIUM

HIRING MATCH GAME

Building your firm's law practice requires that you hire the best
lawyers you can find. This means reading between the lines when
you review resumes. Listed in the left column are resume items.
Match them to what they actually mean in the column on the right.

1. no mention of grades

2. finalist in moot court competition

3. best brief in moot court competition

4. participated in writing competition for law review

5. Phi Alpha Lambda Chi Mu legal fraternity

6. delegate to student bar association

7. *Who's Who in American Colleges and Universities*

a. submitted a lousy paper and was not selected to any journal

b. desperately in need of something to fill in space on resume

c. grandma will be solicited to buy a $50 book real soon (and she'll probably buy it)

d. a glad-hander with little legal ability who will probably be a highly successful lawyer

e. in the bottom 3 percent of class and destined to become a judge

f. selected a brilliant moot court partner who wrote a great brief

g. lost ignominiously in the finals of moot court competition when candidate referred to judge's question as "nitpicky"

[Answers: 1. e; 2. g; 3. f; 4. a; 5. b; 6. d; 7. c]

CLASS ACTION

It's tough to make a living representing single clients, so smart lawyers bring class action suits. The Greenstep Shoe Company recently discovered that it had sent out defective shoes. Can you spot the potential class members for a lawsuit against Greenstep in the picture?

FIND THAT FAX!

They've moved the fax machine again! Can you find its new location? (Hint: one of the senior partners did something to help you find it. Wouldn't it be great if senior partners did that more often?)

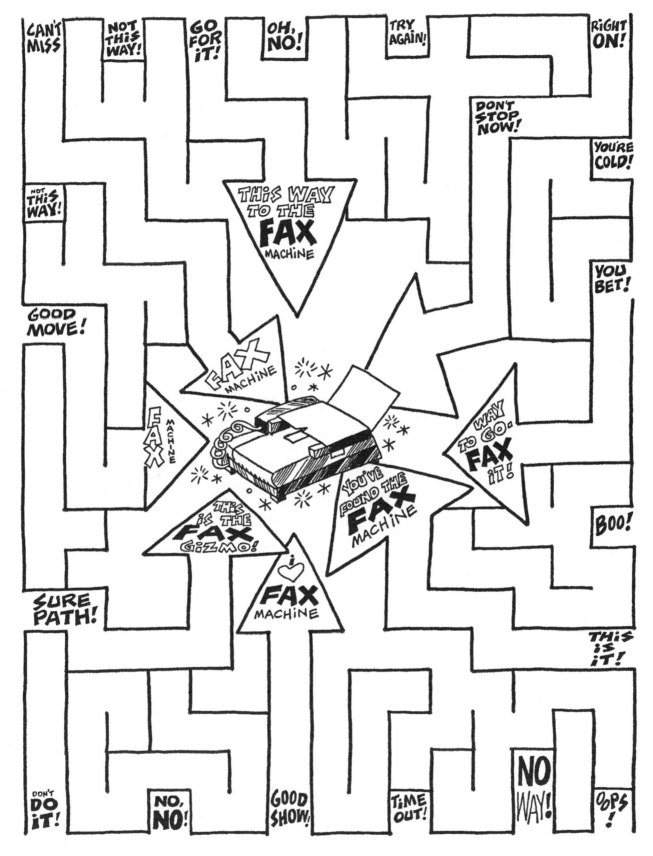

15

PROOFREADING TEST

Mr. Higby is in quite a bind. He sent his memo to the word processing department and it came back with fifteen errors. He wants the memo circulated before noon. Can you help him get it out on schedule?

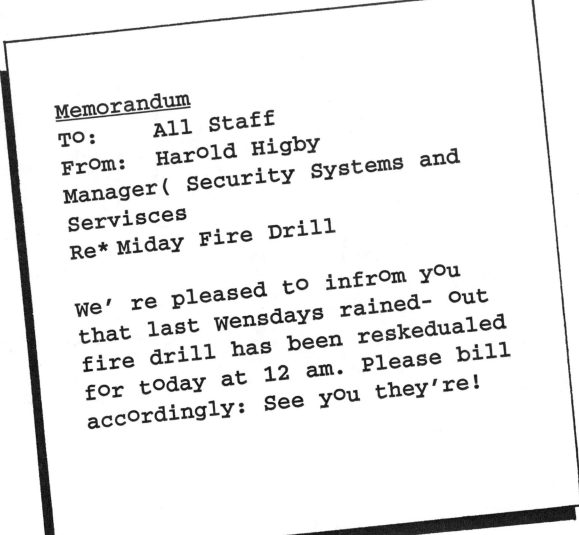

Memorandum

TO: All Staff
FrOm: HarOld Higby
Manager(Security Systems and
Servisces
Re* Miday Fire Drill

We' re pleased to infrOm yOu
that last Wensdays rained- Out
fire drill has been reskedualed
fOr tOday at 12 am. Please bill
accOrdingly: See yOu they're!

WHAT'S THE DIFFERENCE?

One of these modes of communication is different
from the others. Can you tell which one?

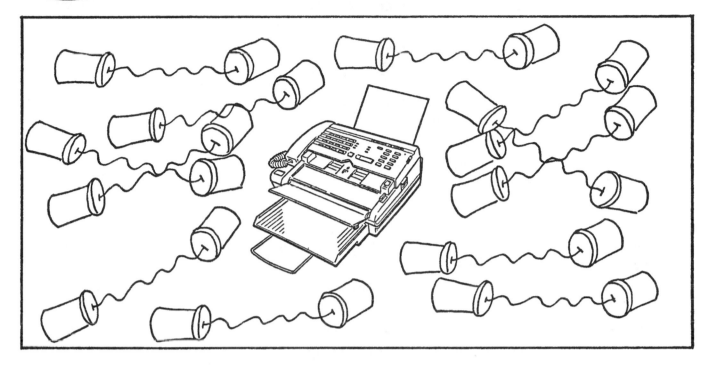

Two of these legal pads are exactly the same. Can you figure out
which two they are?

[Answer: We're still working on it.]

ANSWER THE CLIENT

Your success as a lawyer may depend on how well you handle calls from clients who expect you to come up with spur-of-the-moment advice on subjects entirely outside your area of expertise. This quiz will test your spur-of-the-moment answering ability.

1. Your client Freddie Fitzsimmons owns a gas station. Freddie is considering entering into an agreement with the gas station owner across the street that neither of them will charge less than $1.55 per gallon for regular gasoline. If Freddie asks your advice, you should tell him:
   a. His agreement would clearly violate antitrust laws.
   b. Antitrust laws are complicated and difficult to understand, so his agreement may or may not violate antitrust laws.
   c. There's no problem with the agreement, but you think the price should be $1.60 per gallon.
   d. I'll get back to you on that.

2. Your client Gloria Antwerp just ran into the rear end of a 1994 Rolls-Royce because she was thinking about whether or not to buy a new light green dress she saw at T. J. Maxx. If Gloria asks your advice, you should tell her:
   a. She is absolutely liable for damages to the owner of the Rolls-Royce since she hit the car from behind.
   b. She may have a defense since what was that guy doing driving a car like that in her neighborhood anyway?
   c. She should buy the dress since light green is definitely her color.
   d. I'll get back to you on that.

3. Your client Ann Edwards is president of Iron Industries, Inc. The Environmental Protection Agency has just informed Ann that emissions from the Triple-I factory in Gary, Indiana, are killing the rare side-stroking obswego carp that inhabit the river that runs past the plant. If Ann asks your advice, you should tell her:
   a. You can probably delay the EPA proceedings until all the side-stroking obswegos are dead.
   b. She has absolute liability and will probably be sentenced to two hundred hours of community service working with disadvantaged carp.
   c. She should build a swimming pool near the plant, place all the side-stroking obswegos in the pool, and sell tickets to the public to watch the obswegos race.
   d. I'll get back to you on that.

4. Your client Bob Anderson went to work out at the He-Man Health and Racquet Club. While Bob was in the shower somebody broke into his locker and stole everything. Shortly thereafter Bob was stopped by a policeman who charged him with indecent exposure for making an illegal right turn while driving naked. If Bob asks your advice, you should tell him:
   a. If the judge hears all the facts, he will probably dismiss the case.
   b. If the judge hears all the facts, he will probably die laughing.
   c. You've seen the judge driving naked.
   d. I'll get back to you on that.

[Answers: 1. d; 2. d; 3. d; 4. d]

18

LAWYER TRADING CARDS

Why are there trading cards for third-rate shortstops and not first-rate lawyers? Cut out these cards and trade them with your friends.

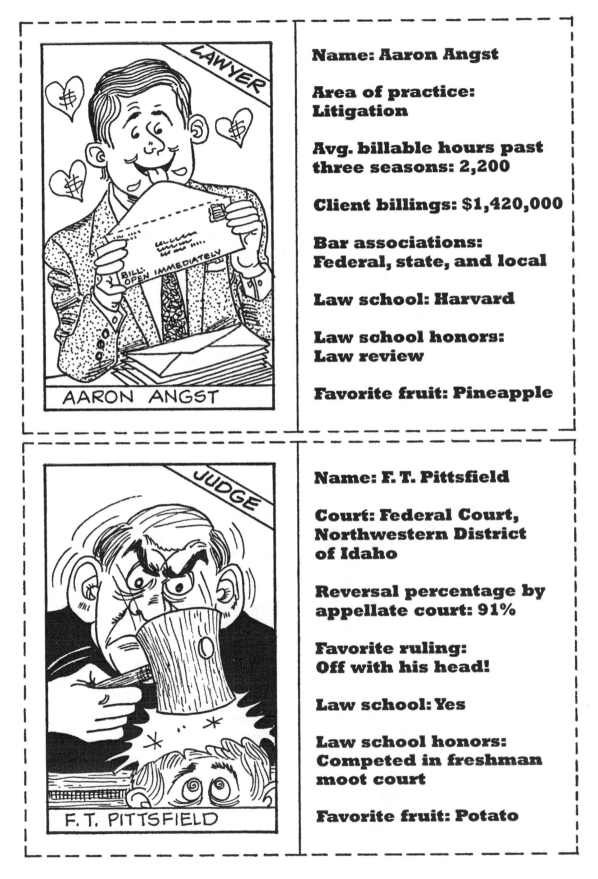

Name: Aaron Angst

Area of practice: Litigation

Avg. billable hours past three seasons: 2,200

Client billings: $1,420,000

Bar associations: Federal, state, and local

Law school: Harvard

Law school honors: Law review

Favorite fruit: Pineapple

Name: F. T. Pittsfield

Court: Federal Court, Northwestern District of Idaho

Reversal percentage by appellate court: 91%

Favorite ruling: Off with his head!

Law school: Yes

Law school honors: Competed in freshman moot court

Favorite fruit: Potato

Name: Betty-Jean Perkins

Area of practice: Trusts and Estates

Avg. billable hours past three seasons: 670

Client billings: $1,350,000

Bar associations: Chair, Committee on Reversionary Interests, Bar of Paris (Texas)

Law school: University of Texas

Law school honors: American Jurisprudence Award, Administrative Law

Favorite fruit: Mango

BETTY-JEAN PERKINS

Name: Get, Rich & Quick

Number of lawyers: 175, give or take 15

Avg. billable hours (associates): 2,350

Avg. billable hours (partners): 1,143

Annual revenues: $107,000,000

Profits per partner: $352,000

GET, RICH & QUICK

THE HIRE TARGET

Making the right hiring decision is not easy. To help you make those tough decisions, paste up this page on a wall in your office. Then have one of your partners blindfold you and spin you around from a distance of twenty feet. Throw a dart at the target and follow the advice you get.

MATCH PIG LATIN TO ENGLISH

For those of you who have trouble with Latin, try pig Latin. Match the
English words in the left column with the pig Latin translation on the right.

1. trial by jury

2. defendant

3. real estate

4. ERISA

5. Contract

6. Order in the Court

7. interrogatory

8. Counsel

a. deroray inay ethay Ourtkay

b. terrogatoryinay

c. ialtray ibay Uryjay

d. Ounselkay

e. efendantday

f. Ontractkay

g. rissa-eay

h. ealray tate-esay

MUSICAL OFFICES

The firm of Flattor, Pandor & Pleez is rearranging its office space. Partners Morgan, Wong, Swansen, and Chavez are getting corner offices. Partners Morgan, Swansen, Cooper, and Lichtenhan must have windows. Partners Wong and Gephart have a dog (Fluffy) and a bird (Einstein), respectively. Gephart is allergic to Fluffy. Einstein is allergic to Swansen. Partners Chavez, Swansen, Lichtenhan, and DiCarlo cannot be in the same room as, respectively, partners Morgan, Swansen, Gephart, and Cooper for even one second. Partner Wong is getting divorced from his wife of seven years, Susie Carpenter-Wong. He is very depressed. What's the fewest number of trips required to accomplish the move?

[Answer: Six]

23

A, I'M AN ATTORNEY!

Another fun game for the car. Fill in the blanks with words starting with *A*, then have your partner do the same with *B*, etc. When you've gotten through the alphabet, try it again!

Here's an example to get you started.

AN "L" OF A PUZZLE

Twelve objects in this picture start with the letter *L*. If you can find
and circle them all, you are a lauded lawyer.

READ THE JURY

An experienced trial lawyer knows how to read a jury and adjusts his case accordingly. You are defending Harry (the Rat) Respot against charges that he robbed the First National Bank of Lower Brooklyn and brutally beat the security guard. Can you identify which jurors are on your side and which are leaning against you?

CONNECT THE DOTS

What picture do they make? Try it upside down! (Extra challenge: time yourself. See if you can take twice as much time as you did the first time. Now apply this principle to increase your billable hours.)

START

1-

2- END

PICTURE THIS

You need some impressive pictures to put on your office credenza to wow the clients. Just paste in photographs from magazines or your family album as indicated.

MAZE PHRASE

Take each letter through the maze to form a famous legal phrase.

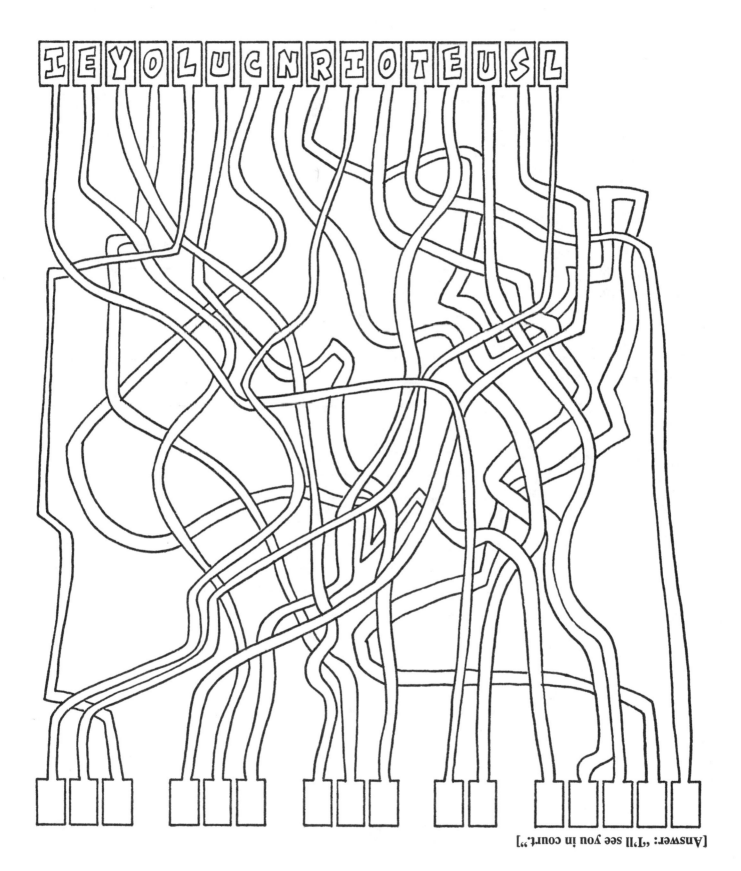

[Answer: "I'll see you in court."]

HOUR POWER: BILL YOUR TIME

Time is money. Any lawyer worth his briefs knows that billable hours have nothing to do with real hours spent on a client matter. Indeed, staying in business depends on the ability to bill creatively. Try your hand at billing these services.

Last Thursday, you

✔ made eight different phone calls to separate clients, each lasting an average of four minutes

✔ called the health club to reserve a racquet-ball court for 9 A.M. next Saturday

✔ drafted an agreement which involved filling in six blanks in a form contract you've been using for years

✔ spent three hours breathing into a paper bag to rid yourself of a nasty case of the hiccups

✔ spent two and a half hours preparing a bill for a client

✔ went to the dentist for your annual checkup

Fill in the time sheet to show your billable hours for the day.

MATTER AND DESCRIPTION	NUMBER OF HOURS
TOTAL NUMBER OF HOURS	

[Answers: 0–5 hours—find another profession; 6–8 hours—useful associate; 9–12 hours—partnership material; 13–24 hours—disbarment material]

30

ANALOGIES

If you liked the SAT, the LSAT, and the bar exam, you'll love these analogy questions written especially for lawyers.

1. STATUS: LAWYER

    a. status:doctor

    b. status:teacher

    c. paper clip:White-Out

    d. Mama chimp:Baby chimp

2. CLIENT: BILL

    a. client:Jane

    b. gray:purple

    c. umpire:rule

    d. *Melrose Place:Beverly Hills 90210*

3. QUESTION: WITNESS

    a. queen of hearts:tarts

    b. queen of hearts:torts

    c. chess:checkers

    d. judge:jury

[Answers: 1. d; 2. b; 3. c]

DOWNSIZE YOUR FIRM

Not everybody you hire works out. Some of the lawyers below need to be downsized out of your firm. Identify those lawyers, cut them out, and throw them in the wastebasket.

1. Adam Ackerman billed 2,500 hours last year and brought in $1 million in new business.
2. Barbara Brant billed 2,700 hours and did high-quality work. At the firm party, she offended the managing partner by calling his wife "a little harlot."
3. Charles Carew billed 2,200 hours last year. 2,100 of those hours were billed to pro bono clients for which the firm received no fees.
4. Denise Donale billed 1,100 hours. She is not very smart. Her father, Doctor Donale, is president and chief executive officer of Presumed Parasites, a firm client that paid $2 million in legal fees last year.
5. Edward Evers billed 1,300 hours last year. He's the firm's only expert in ERISA. Edward also called the managing partner's spouse "a little harlot" at the firm party.

[Answer: So long, Babs and Chuck.]

32

PIN THE BRANCH OFFICE ON THE MAP

Puzzled about where to locate your new international branch office? It's simple.
Cut out the circles and back them with double-sided tape. Hang the map on the
wall and spin each partner around three times. Partners then walk up to the
board with eyes closed. The one who gets the most branch offices on the map—
excluding bodies of water—wins.

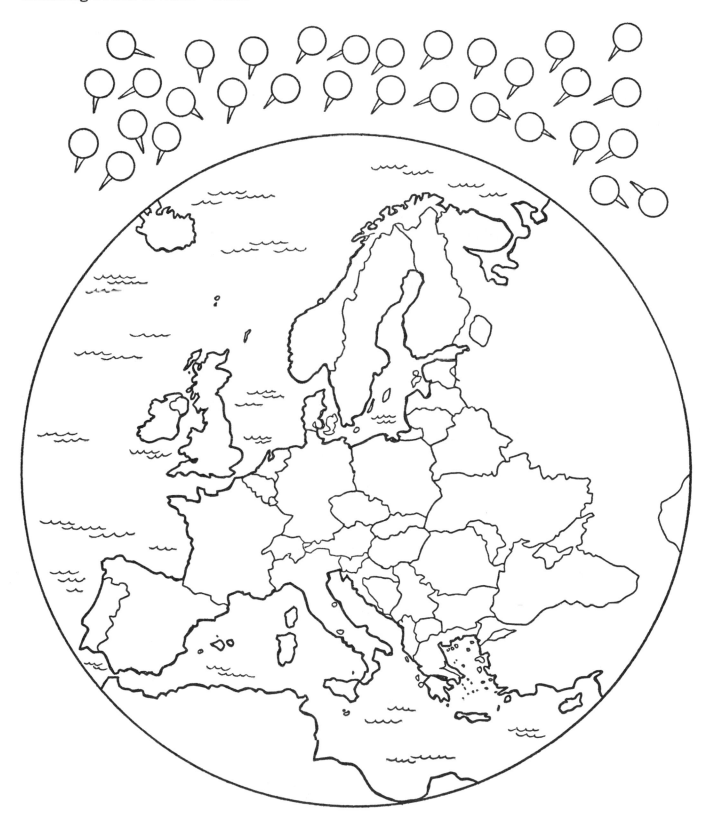

WHICH ONE WAS WRITTEN BY THE LAWYER?

Lawyers have a distinct writing style. Below are three letters asking special people important questions. Can you pick out the one written by the lawyer?

Darling,
I can't sleep. I can't eat. I can't breathe. I ache for you
more fervently with each passing year. Will you see me
again? I am entirely yours,
Leon

Scotty:
Let's play dragons again tomorrow, OK?
I think you're a really good fire-breather.
Bye. Love,
    Josie

```
To:    Ellen P. Burrows
From:  Richard R. Silton
Re:    Holy Matrimony
cc:    Mrs. Ethel S. Silton
```

I am writing to request your presence before God and selected guests at a public ceremony. At said ceremony, Ellen P. Burrows (hereinafter referred to as "Proposee") would agree to be bound to Richard R. Silton (hereinafter referred to as "Proposer") in holy matrimony, in sickness and in health, as long as Proposee and Proposer both shall live, unless sooner terminated by no-fault divorce. Proposee and Proposer would agree upon hyphenation of last names and other critical matters prior to attendance at said ceremony. I would appreciate your prompt attention to this matter.

RRS: mvp

HOTEL TREASURE HUNT

Here are pictures of some fun items you can find around your hotel. Race your traveling partners to see who can place the real items on top of the pictures first. Ready, set, go!

CLIENT FISHING

Hooking clients is a tough job. Which of the lawyers in the boat has hooked the client?

[Answer: We're not really sure.]

ALTERNATIVE DISPUTE RESOLUTION

The cost of bringing a case to trial has become so great that clients and lawyers now search diligently for alternative methods to resolve disputes. Name the alternative dispute resolution methods used by the people in this picture.

WHICH WAY ARE THE BOOKS?

 This is Susie Johnson's first day as a new associate. She's in a terrible tizzy because she can't find the library. Can you help Susie?

HOW TO LEAVE YOUR OFFICE LOOKING AS IF YOU'RE BUSY

Second-year associate Roxanne Dolt left the office at 4 P.M. to have a drink (well, let's be honest, several drinks) and go bowling. Place the items in the margins of this page in the appropriate place in the picture so that Roxy's senior partner Richard "Skip" Partridge III will think Roxy just stepped out for a minute.

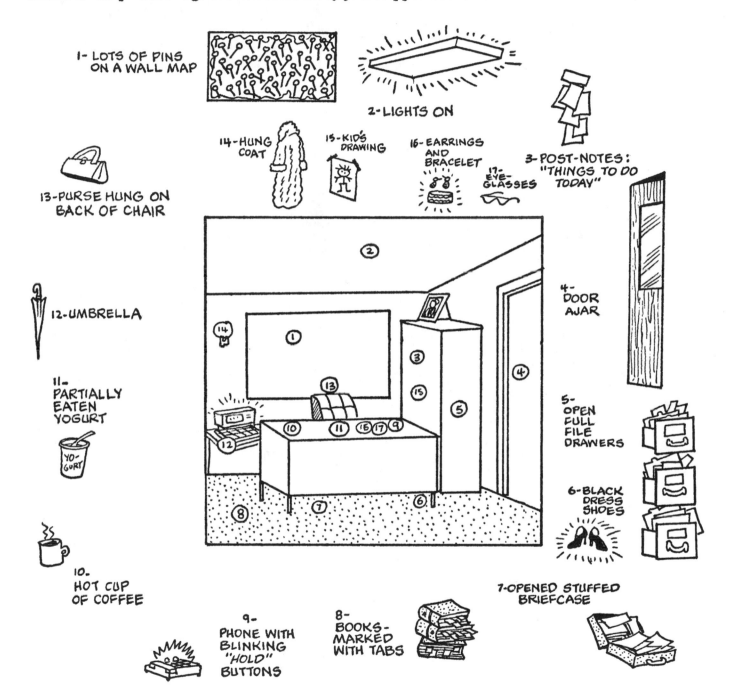

HOLDING COURT

Nine members of the U.S. Supreme Court have gone to see Amazing
Mindy play the accordion. Can you find them in this picture?

PICK A CARD

Too many lawyers use stodgy old business cards and miss the opportunity to distinguish themselves. Here are some suggestions you may adapt (steal) when you design your firm's business card.

LAWYER POETRY

Lawyers are sometimes thought of as dull and unimaginative. That's a bum rap. Accountants are dull and unimaginative; lawyers are just dull. In fact, some of the world's greatest poets were lawyers—Lord Byron and Harvey Glickstein, for two. To prove that lawyers are romantics at heart, complete the following poems with the words at the right:

Roses are red
Violets are blue
Attorneys are sweet
Even when they _____ .

There was a young lady from Port
Who plied her trades in the court.
Though she knew how to plead,
Ex contractu if need,
Her favorite action was_____ .

I think that I shall never see
A poem expensive as a
lawyer's _____ .

'Twas brillig, and the slithy toves
    Did gyre and gimble in the wabe:
All mimsy were the borogroves,
    And the mome raths_____ .

The woods are lovely, dark and deep,
But I have courtroom dates to keep,
And _____ before I sleep,
And _____ before I sleep.

sue

hours to bill

tort

hours to bill

fee

outgrabe

REJECTION CAN BE FUN!

Write a rejection letter to a law student using the
following phrases:

- ✗ **your fine record**
- ✗ **many qualified applicants**
- ✗ **lead a horse to water**
- ✗ **fish out of water**
- ✗ **water under the bridge**
- ✗ **four out of five dentists**
- ✗ **that's life**
- ✗ **keep in touch**

HARD DAY

Hard day at work? Encounter an ungrateful client? An inconsiderate partner? Lose a big case? Cut out this rubber ducky. He'll comfort you. And tomorrow you'll knock 'em dead at the office!

44

FIND THE HIDDEN CLIENTS

Successful lawyers can identify people in their day-to-day environment who might need their services. Twenty potential clients are shown in this picture. Can you find the clients and identify the parties to be sued?

AIRPLANE TREASURE HUNT

Here's a list of fun items to collect on an airplane. Race your travel partners to see who can collect them all first. Seat belts fastened? Three, two, one, take-off!

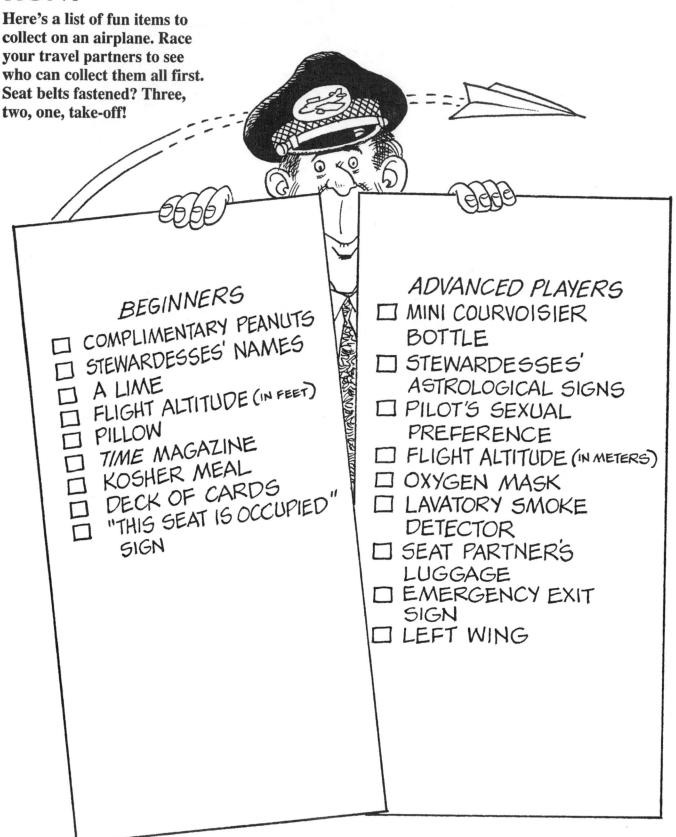

BEGINNERS
- ☐ COMPLIMENTARY PEANUTS
- ☐ STEWARDESSES' NAMES
- ☐ A LIME
- ☐ FLIGHT ALTITUDE (IN FEET)
- ☐ PILLOW
- ☐ *TIME* MAGAZINE
- ☐ KOSHER MEAL
- ☐ DECK OF CARDS
- ☐ "THIS SEAT IS OCCUPIED" SIGN

ADVANCED PLAYERS
- ☐ MINI COURVOISIER BOTTLE
- ☐ STEWARDESSES' ASTROLOGICAL SIGNS
- ☐ PILOT'S SEXUAL PREFERENCE
- ☐ FLIGHT ALTITUDE (IN METERS)
- ☐ OXYGEN MASK
- ☐ LAVATORY SMOKE DETECTOR
- ☐ SEAT PARTNER'S LUGGAGE
- ☐ EMERGENCY EXIT SIGN
- ☐ LEFT WING

"B" CAREFUL

Betty Broadhurst of Boston is in a big rush. She needs to bicycle over to the Barrister Building on Broadway to argue her case before Judge Bob Bigwig. Help Betty travel through this bewildering maze by stepping only on boxes containing objects that begin with the letter *B*. You can move only horizontally and vertically. Best of luck!

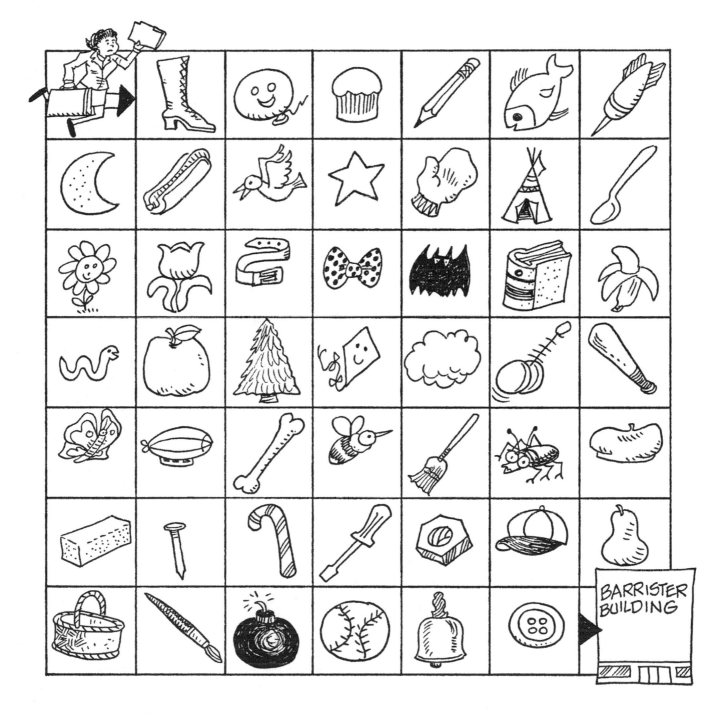

LAWYER-CLIENT MATCH

Can you match the lawyers below with their clients?

- ☐ criminal lawyer
- ☐ personal injury lawyer
- ☐ real estate lawyer
- ☐ sports lawyer
- ☐ bankruptcy lawyer
- ☐ public interest lawyer
- ☐ entertainment lawyer

a   b   c   d   e   f   g

| 1 CRIMINAL LAWYER | 2 REAL ESTATE LAWYER | 3 PUBLIC INTEREST LAWYER | 4 ENTERTAINMENT LAWYER | 5 SPORTS LAWYER | 6 BANKRUPTCY LAWYER | 7 PERSONAL INJURY LAWYER |

[Answers: 1, a; 2, c; 3, f; 4, g; 5, d; 6, e; 7, b]

48

VERY SIMPLE CROSSWORD PUZZLE

 Been out of law school a while? Don't worry—you still speak law like a native. To prove it, cross-examine yourself on these obscure citations.

Across

2. The law says you have to stop when you come to this color traffic light, even if you're in a big hurry.

3. "The truth, the whole truth, and nothing ____ the truth."

Down

1. "Life, liberty, ____ the pursuit of happiness."

2. The law says you can't do this to a bank with panty hose over your head.

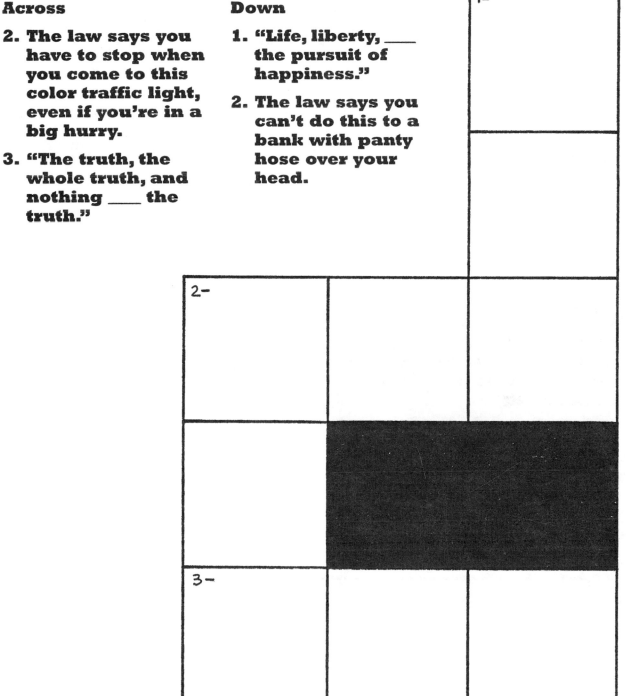

BILLING BIG

Nothing builds confidence like sending out a seven-figure bill. But how many lawyers get to do that? Not many. Now *you* can! Just cut out the bill below and send it to us.

YOUR FIRM'S NAME AND ADDRESS

Arnold B. Kanter and Jodi I. Kanter
c/o San Diego Zoo
Reptile House
8th Floor
820 Loco Blvd.
San Diego, CA 92929

Date

For legal services rendered in connection with completing or trying to complete various of the items contained in *The Lawyer's Big Book of Fun*, including, inter alia, puzzles, coloring, connect the dots, etc.	$1,700,000.00
Expenses Postage	$ .32
Total Due	$1,700,000.32

Note: We won't pay the bill, but neither would your client.

SPELL-THE-PHRASE MAZE

See if you can travel through this maze by correctly spelling the phrase "Ignorance of the law is no defense."

TIME MANAGEMENT QUIZ

To be an effective lawyer, you have to manage your time effectively. Follow Godfrey Bleschieu through his day in the following story. Where indicated, write your suggestions for making Godfrey's day more productive.

Godfrey Bleschieu arrives at his office building at seven-thirty. He gets on the elevator with Chris, a senior associate at the firm. Chris would like to get Godfrey's advice for a brief Chris is preparing in a matter which has issues similar to those Godfrey dealt with in another case. Godfrey suggests they meet in Chris's office at ten-thirty. [1._____]

As he passes the reception area, Godfrey grabs the latest *Sports Illustrated* (the swimsuit issue), leafs through it, and crashes into Gary Swath. Swath picks himself up from the carpet and asks Godfrey's advice on a litigation matter. Godfrey says, "Sure, call me later. But, you know, wait a sec, I think a case just came down from the Supreme Court. Let's go to the library and see if we can find it in the advance sheets." Godfrey and Gary proceed to the library where, after half an hour, they locate the Supreme Court case that Godfrey was thinking of. It has no bearing on Gary's case. [2._____]

Back in his office, Godfrey begins returning phone calls from the stack of messages on his desk. Many of those people are not in now, so Godfrey leaves messages. He forgets all about the ten-thirty meeting with Chris and has to reschedule it for the afternoon. He reviews the morning mail and dictates responses to his secretary. [3._____]

Godfrey consumes a sandwich at his desk and starts to prepare notes for a negotiation session in New York. Pat, a senior associate in Godfrey's department, drops by his office to ask "a quick question that just came up on a very important matter" for Godfrey's biggest client. Pat, who has been handling the project alone, spends ten minutes laying out the background. Godfrey answers the question, which was pure common sense that any idiot could have figured out in less than a minute. [4._____]

Godfrey's secretary informs him that he's been asked to attend a practice group meeting about the training needs of associates. When the meeting concludes an hour later, Godfrey returns telephone calls to people who returned his calls. Then he revises the drafts of correspondence he dictated earlier. [5._____]

Godfrey realizes that he has to leave for the airport in twenty minutes, so he goes to the bookstore in the basement of the building to pick up a trashy novel for the plane. Exhausted, he leaves for the airport on time but gets caught in traffic and misses his flight to New York. [6._____]

Answers:

1. Do not ride up (or down) in an elevator with anybody from the firm.

2. Refuse to help firm colleagues with their problems.

3. Ignore e-mail and phone calls; if it's that important, they'll call back.

4. Fire Pat.

5. Forget about continuing legal education for associates on the theory that "If I got along without it, so can they—especially with what we pay them."

6. Get an associate to handle the New York negotiation.

52

HIRING THE BEST

To attract the best law students, you have to produce a brochure that contains all the clichés of lawyer recruitment. Prepare a page for the brochure of Weel Getcha & Nailia which uses the following phrases:

- cutting-edge work
- camaraderie
- a penny saved is a penny earned
- excellent support staff
- an eye for an eye, a tooth for a tooth
- pay the going rate
- training second to none
- mares eat oats and does eat oats, and little lambs eat ivy

FANCY LETTERHEAD

To impress clients, you need a fancy letterhead. Design a letterhead
for Rothengasser & Jones using these elements:

Rothengasser & Jones

Samuel Jones

Wilhelmina Jones

Albert Jones

Richard Jones

Edward "Chick" Jones

F. W. Jones

Joan Jones

Ulysses Jones

Russell Jones

Jo Ellyn Jones

Hugh Jones

Gary & Denise Jones

Floyd Jones

T. R. Jones

R. T. Jones

R. T. Jones, Jr.

Effie Jones

Jones Moving & Storage

Kurt Jones

Zachary Jones

Calvin B. Rothengasser XI

Rio de Janeiro

Des Moines

Beijing

Milan

Gary

Sydney

Oslo

Budapest

Quito

Bangkok

Bombay

Topeka

Writer's direct dial
number: (unlisted)

Famous since 1991

Counselors at Law and
Equity

Warning from the
Surgeon General: legal
fees may be dangerous to
your financial health

BRIEFCASE PUZZLE

It's one thing to have everything you need to look lawyerly. But
where do you put it all? Which of these items would you put into
your briefcase? Make sure the briefcase closes!

HOTEL OBSTACLE COURSE

Don't let being cooped up in a stuffy hotel room on a business trip be an obstacle to fun! Time yourself over courses such as this one:

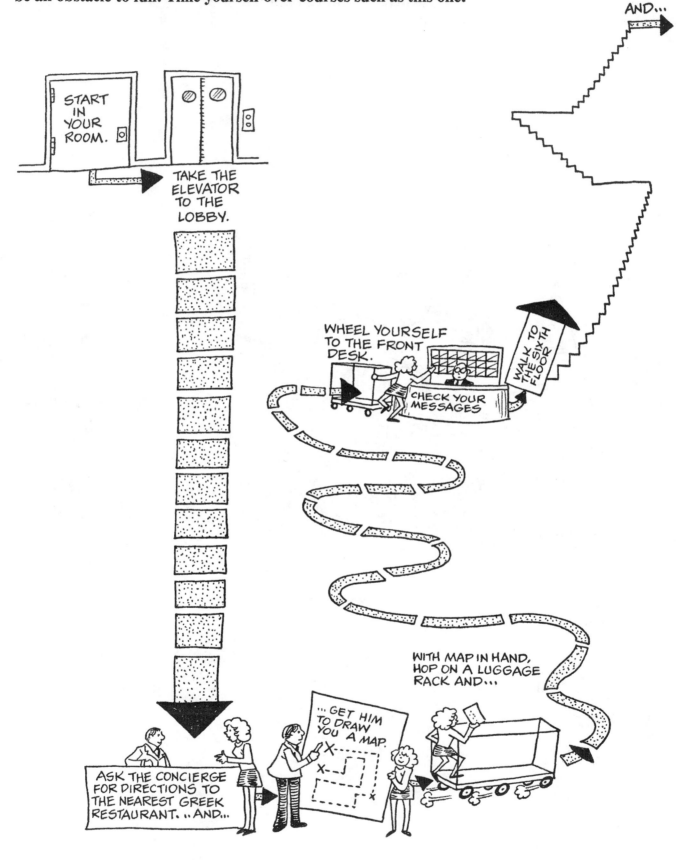

START IN YOUR ROOM.

TAKE THE ELEVATOR TO THE LOBBY.

WHEEL YOURSELF TO THE FRONT DESK.

CHECK YOUR MESSAGES

WALK TO THE SIXTH FLOOR

AND...

WITH MAP IN HAND, HOP ON A LUGGAGE RACK AND...

... GET HIM TO DRAW YOU A MAP.

ASK THE CONCIERGE FOR DIRECTIONS TO THE NEAREST GREEK RESTAURANT. ...AND...

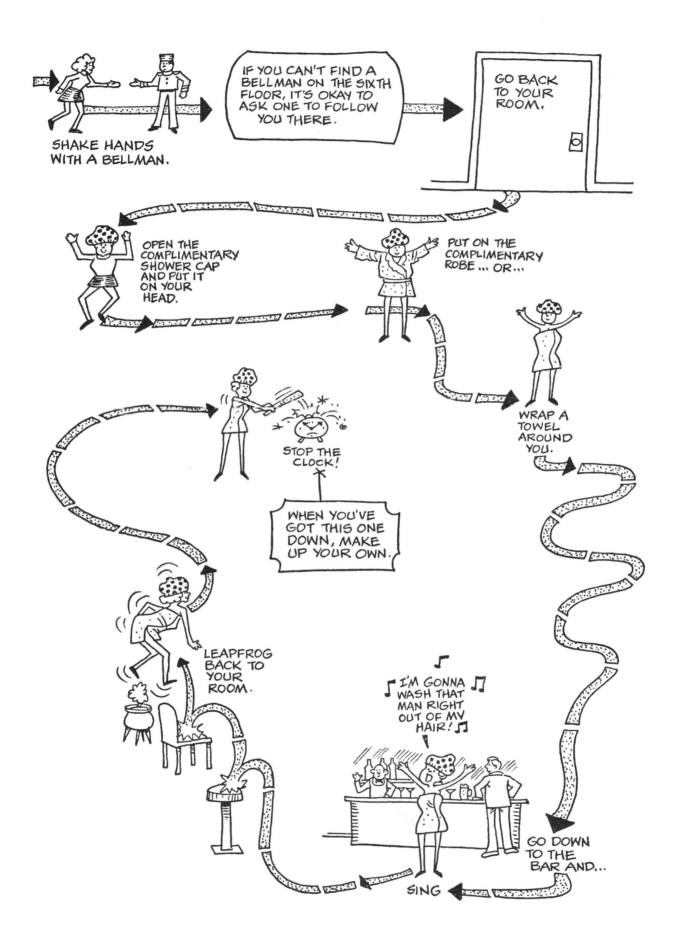

TRACK THE KILLER

Famous criminal lawyer Charles Clibourn can get the case against his client dismissed if he can follow the trail of the real murderer, Horrible Harry. Horrible Harry has only four toes on his foot. Can you help Charles track down Horrible Harry?

AFTER HOURS

Use this page to draw a picture of what your office looks like on a dark night with all the lights out. Don't be afraid to use whatever imagination you still have left after law school. (Note to estate planners: forget about imagination.)

FIND THE KIDS

Today is Family Day at the law firm of Arwee Aftafees & How. Charlie the clown is entertaining the children. Larry Arwee's seven offspring all wear baseball caps with the letter *A*. Larry is sick of watching Charlie and wants to go home. Can you help Larry find his kids?

ENHANCE YOUR RESUME

Since the market is so unstable these days, you'll probably leave your present job a lot sooner than you think. For a great new job, you need an impressive resume. As practice, revise this resume to make Samantha Leigh Rosen more marketable. (See next page for sample revision.)

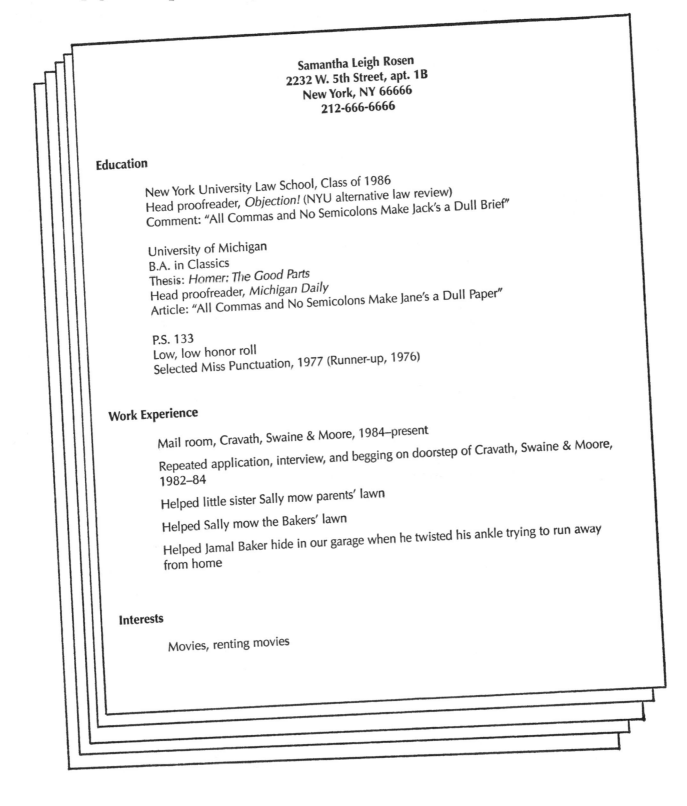

Samantha Leigh Rosen
2232 W. 5th Street, apt. 1B
New York, NY 66666
212-666-6666

Education

New York University Law School, Class of 1986
Head proofreader, *Objection!* (NYU alternative law review)
Comment: "All Commas and No Semicolons Make Jack's a Dull Brief"

University of Michigan
B.A. in Classics
Thesis: *Homer: The Good Parts*
Head proofreader, *Michigan Daily*
Article: "All Commas and No Semicolons Make Jane's a Dull Paper"

P.S. 133
Low, low honor roll
Selected Miss Punctuation, 1977 (Runner-up, 1976)

Work Experience

Mail room, Cravath, Swaine & Moore, 1984–present

Repeated application, interview, and begging on doorstep of Cravath, Swaine & Moore, 1982–84

Helped little sister Sally mow parents' lawn

Helped Sally mow the Bakers' lawn

Helped Jamal Baker hide in our garage when he twisted his ankle trying to run away from home

Interests

Movies, renting movies

S. Leigh Rosen VI
2232 W. 5th Street, Suite 1B
New York, NY 66666
pager #212-338-7170
car phone: 212-ROS-ENVI

Education

New York University Law School, Class of 1986
Editor-in-Chief, Law Review*
Comment: "Levis and DNA: The Patentability of Jeans and Genes."**

University of Michigan
B.A. in Classics, summa cum fortuna
Thesis: *Homer: The Author and the Man*

P.S. 133
Graduated in top 90 percent of class
Lettered in track, soccer, softball, basketball, badminton, and curling
Selected Most Outstanding Graduate in the History of the School,
    1902–present

Work Experience

Associated with Cravath, Swaine & Moore, 1984–present

Joined budding lawn mowing business in high school and doubled
    company's profits, customer base

Established nonprofit shelter and hospital for the disabled and homeless

Interests

Dog training, hammer-dulcimer playing, reverse bungee-jumping, karachi

*roommate of
**cite-checked

WHO'S THE FUTURE LAWYER?

Early on, kids show natural aptitudes for certain professions. Future architects build sandcastles, future soldiers play GI Joe, and future senators play doctor. Can you pick out the future lawyer in this nursery school classroom?

POCKET SECRETARY

Can't find your secretary when you want her—or him? Well, those days are gone for good. Simply cut out the secretary of your choice below, fold her/him up—and you'll never be without a secretary again.

FOLD HERE

FOLD HERE

FOLD HERE

FOLD HERE

FOLD HERE

FOLD HERE

LAWYER TIC-TAC-TOE

Important lawyers fax frequently. "But," you may say, "I don't always have something to fax." Fortunately, that doesn't matter! Try this: make the first move on the tic-tac-toe board below. (You can choose either *X*s or *O*s, but not both.) Then fax your move to a lawyer in another city and wait for the response. (Note: you can do this *all day long!*)

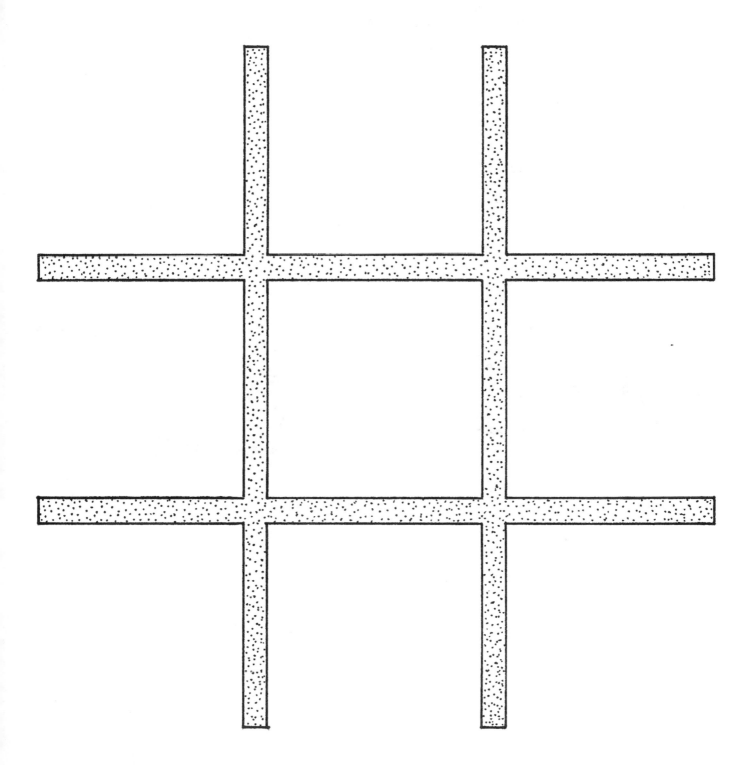

FREQUENT-FLIER MILES

The goal of the traveling businessperson is to accumulate frequent-flier miles and save time and money. The goal of the traveling lawyer is to accumulate frequent-flier miles and bill time. (Money's no object.) You are a lawyer. You need to fly from Chicago to New York, and you have two choices. Select the best route.

1. Chicago to New York nonstop on American Airlines. (Time: 2 hours; cost: $250; frequent-flier miles: 780.)

2. Chicago to Fort Wayne, Indiana. Fort Wayne to Indianapolis. Indianapolis to Cleveland. Cleveland to Columbus. Columbus to Pittsburgh. Pittsburgh to Philadelphia. Philadelphia to Chicago. Chicago to New York. (Time: 36 hours; cost: $1,940; frequent-flier miles: [with bonuses] 6,250.)

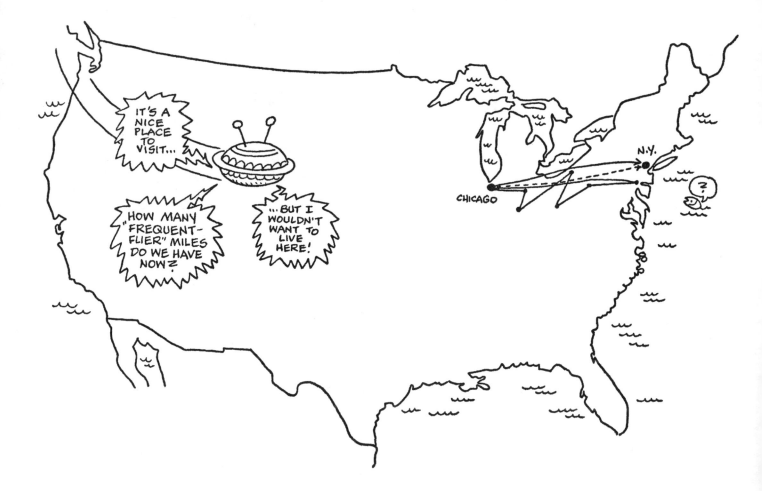

AMAZING LETTERS

See if you can find your way through this letter maze by correctly spelling the phrase "innocent until proven guilty."

MARKETING MAGIC

Tired of that hackneyed promotional language? Distinguish your firm! Design a lead-in paragraph to your firm marketing brochure using the following phrases:

- money-saving
- service-oriented
- international
- oh my gosh
- cutting edge
- infrastructure
- talented
- experienced
- banana
- green
- right foot

OUR EXECUTIVE COMMITTEE DISCUSSES ANOTHER IMPORTANT ISSUE.

KNOW YOUR TELEPHONE

Telephones are so complicated these days. This quiz helps you learn some of the more obscure features of your phone system.

1. Speed Dial provides easy access to

    a. Your barber or beautician

    b. The weather forecast

    c. Your largest client

2. When you use the Last Number Dialed feature, you automatically reach the person you called last. This person is likely to be

    a. The person you last remember talking to

    b. A very important client who is on an international call on his other line and just asked if you could get back to him after lunch

    c. Your grandmother, to whom you have just made your weekly call and who responds, "Betsy, is that you again? Oh, I'm so glad. You are not gonna believe what just happened to me . . ."

    d. Ticked off that you've called again

3. The Speaker feature allows you to

    a. Sound like you are spelunking and have been reached in Carlsbad Caverns

    b. Keep both hands free to play wastebasketball

    c. Retire, since, having attained it, there is nothing more to aspire to

4. This feature allows you to order filet mignon:

    a. Conference Call

    b. Call Transfer

    c. E-Mail

5. This feature is useful when you want to avoid someone and make it look like a technological error:

    a. Conference Call

    b. Call Transfer

    c. Call Forward

    d. Call Park

    e. A taped recording of a fire drill

    f. Hanging up

[Answers:
1. a, b;
2. b, c, d;
3. all of the above;
4. none of the above (actually, the answer is Room Service);
5. all of the above]

IN THE LINE TO FIRE

Play this one with a friend. Here's how: Ask your friend to give you a word of the type listed next to the first blank. (Don't read the sentence—just ask for a word.) Fill in the answer. Keep going till you've completed the whole story. Then read it out loud. (Your friend *should* laugh. If he starts to cry, tell him that the story is made up and that you doubt this will ever happen to him or anyone he loves.)

_____(name 1) was a senior partner and didn't have time to beat

around the _____(noun). "I think you'd better have a _____(noun)," s/he

told _____(name 2), but before s/he did, the words were out: "You're fired."

"Fired?" gasped _____(name 2), dabbing her/his forehead

_____(adverb) with a small _____(noun). "But what for? I meet dead-

lines, I work overtime, I even bring you your _____(noun) every morning."

"Frankly, _____(name 2), we don't like your _____(body part)."

"But that's blatant discrimination! I'll take you to court! I'll sue your

_____(article of clothing) off! And I'll win so fast you won't have time to

say _____(slogan or saying)."

"I wouldn't try that if I were you, _____(pet name). _____(name 3),

_____(name 4) & _____(name 5) has a flawless record of

nondiscrimination. If I were you, I'd _____(verb) along quickly and quietly."

"Okay," _____(name 2) said, and sniffled softly. But s/he was faking

it. On her/his way out, s/he felt for the _____(noun) in her/his pocket.

Back at her/his desk, s/he phoned her/his secretary. "Hold my

_____(plural noun), would you? I don't want to be disturbed. I'm getting

started on some very important research."

DICTATING IS FUN

You're not much of a lawyer if you can't dictate. Practice on this letter. Then turn the page upside down to see the way most lawyers would dictate this letter.

Joseph Chrisahowski
Seven World Trade Tower
New York, NY 20048

Dear Joe:

I have yours of the eighteenth instanter, in which you argue that my client should be barred by the doctrine of res judicata and equitable estoppel from claiming that your client is not entitled to both compensatory and punitive damages for anticipatory breach of contract. I think that, if you bother to research the law on this case, you will find that <u>Lyons</u> v. <u>Class of Morons</u> is dispositive of the issue you raise.

I trust that we will not have to contend with further dilatory tactics in this matter and that we can proceed as originally intended!

With fond regards to you and Marybeth,

I remain yours very truly,

Joseph Chrisahowski: Seven World Trade Tower New York NY 20048 Dear Joe (J-O-E) I have yours of (O-F) the eighteenth instanter comma in which you argue that my client should be barred by the doctrine of res judicata (look that up in Black's if you're not sure of the spelling) and equitable estoppel (by the way, date this next Thursday) from claiming (C-L-A-I-M-I-N-G) that your client is not entitled (by the way, this should be on firm letterhead) to both compensatory and punitive damages for anticipatory breach of contract (I want an extra-wide margin on this, OK?) I think that comma if you bother to research the law on this case comma you will find that Lyons v. Class of Morons under-lined is dispositive of the issue you raise period paragraph I trust that we will not have to contend with further tactics in this matter (make that silly tactics in this matter—no—dilatory tactics . . . uh, where was I? Oh, right—) and that we can proceed as originally intended exclamation point paragraph with fond regards to you and Marybeth (Find out if Marybeth is one word or two; I can never remember) comma paragraph I remain yours very truly comma and then put my name

INSTANT PARTNERSHIP

Write yourself into the firm name! Don't forget to start with a capital letter. Now go ahead and hang out your shingle. Feel pretty important? Good for you!

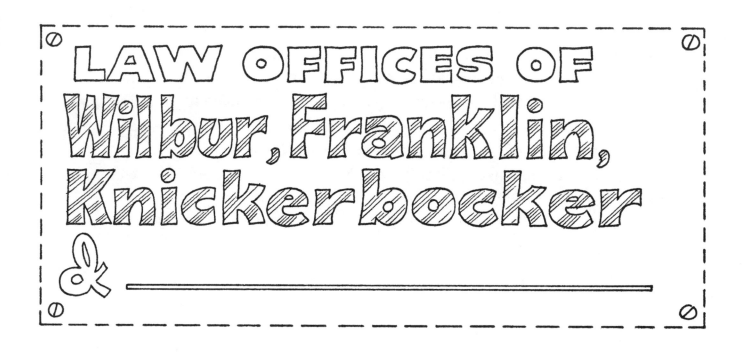

LAW OFFICES OF
Wilbur, Franklin,
Knickerbocker
& _____

PLAYING THE NUMBERS

Using the color code below, paint this picture, frame it, and hang it on the wall right next to your law diploma.

Color code:
1–white
2–black
3–puce
4–vermillion
5–okra

BILLING

BILLING

PAPER CLIP SHUFFLEBOARD

This game can be played by two or more lawyers. The object is to flip the paper clip with your index finger from the place indicated into the target. Each player receives four paper clips per chucker. Six chuckers constitute a game. Your score is determined by where the narrow end of the paper clip lands. Players may try to knock other players out of the target area. Players alternate going first each chucker. This is a game requiring little athletic ability or brains and thus is a favorite of real estate lawyers.

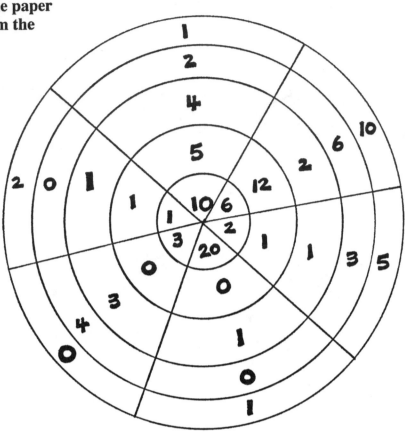

AIRPLANE CRASH

You know the old saying that good luck comes to those who are ready for it? Well, few people are more aware of this than personal injury lawyers. Now, nobody likes to see a plane crash. But if one has to go down, *you* might as well handle some of the cases. However, in order to do that, you must act quickly. Cut out and fold the paper airplane. Cut out the little man and put him on the airplane. Now fly the plane as far as you can. When it crashes, run to the little man and hand him your business card. Keep practicing until you can get to the crash site within fifteen seconds of impact.

FOLD HERE

FOLD HERE

FOLD HERE

FOLD HERE

FOLD HERE

PAPER CLIP

STICK 'EM UP

The greatest invention since fire and the wheel is the little stick-em notes for important messages to yourself and others. As you know, those notes come in different sizes, colors, and shapes. See if you can fill up this page with the types of stick-em notes indicated below. Write up several of each so that they'll be ready to go next time you need them.

STATUS SYMBOLS

Lawyers thrive on prestige. Unless you can recognize prestige, you are not likely to make it big. See if you can find the status symbols in the picture.

WHITE OUT EVIL

A lot of evil forces are after lawyers these days. Even nonparanoid lawyers think so. Fortunately there is a weapon available to fight those evil forces—White-Out. Take your bottle of White-Out and eliminate the evil that threatens the lawyers in this picture.

TOOT YOUR HORN

When you're good, word gets out . . . eventually . . . sometimes . . .
But why chance it? Prepare your own press release, touting your
accomplishments. Include these words:

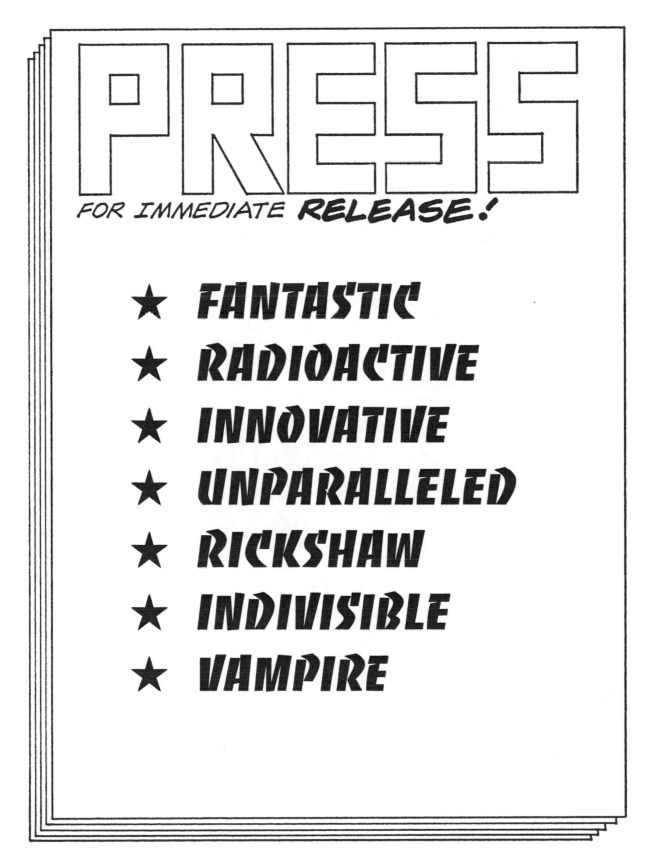

PRESS

FOR IMMEDIATE RELEASE!

★ **FANTASTIC**

★ **RADIOACTIVE**

★ **INNOVATIVE**

★ **UNPARALLELED**

★ **RICKSHAW**

★ **INDIVISIBLE**

★ **VAMPIRE**

COLORING

Color the picture on this page and paste it up in your office. Be sure to stay inside the lines.

PLANNING FOR RETIREMENT

You certainly don't want to be a lawyer forever, do you? But just how long will you have to work to guarantee comfortable retirement? Use the worksheet to calculate when you can retire.

Retirement WORKSHEET

1. age at which you plan to die ⎯⎯⎯

2. subtract age at which you plan to retire ⎯⎯⎯

3. number of years you will spend in retirement ⎯⎯⎯

4. current expenses per year x 390% (adjusted for inflation) ⎯⎯⎯

5. amount you'll need for retirement (multiply line 3 by line 4) ⎯⎯⎯

6. subtract current assets ⎯⎯⎯

7. add current liabilities ⎯⎯⎯

8. add $2 million for unexpected expenses ⎯⎯⎯

9. add amount of alimony you will have to pay to your spouse ⎯⎯⎯

10. subtract social security payments anticipated ⎯⎯⎯

11. add social security payments anticipated (by the time you retire there won't be any social security) ⎯⎯⎯

12. subtract your projected savings (not less than zero) per year from now until retirement x number of years between now and retirement ⎯⎯⎯

13. number of years you must work until retirement ⎯⎯⎯

[Answer: Forget it—you're going to die with your boots on.]

PUTTING THINGS TOGETHER

Somebody has carelessly ripped up the money your client brought in to pay your bill. Can you cut out the pieces and paste them together again?

FUN WITH THE PHOTOCOPY MACHINE

Overworked and underpaid? Underpaid? Get serious. Try this fun game with your photocopy machine to reduce stress and enlarge your salary.

PHONEY TUNES

Have you ever noticed that the numbers on your telephone make different sounds? To see how this works, call your biggest client, hang up, and then call your significant other. The numbers play different tunes, don't they? They don't? Uh-oh. . . . Here's a phone activity you will enjoy. First, check to see that no one else is in easy listening range of your office. Then pick up your phone and try to play these songs:

- *"HAPPY BIRTHDAY"*
- *"MARY HAD A LITTLE LAMB"*
- *"YOU AIN'T NOTHIN' BUT A HOUND DOG"*
- *"MOONLIGHT SONATA"*

Once you've got them down, play them backward and listen for satanic messages!

FIND THE LAWYER

An important part of your success as a lawyer is being able to deal with other lawyers. To do that, you've first got to identify them. See if you can pick out the lawyer in the accompanying picture.

WHAT'S WRONG WITH THIS PICTURE?

Can you find twelve things wrong in this picture?

GETTING THE MESSAGE

As a lawyer, you are judged largely by the company you keep. Therefore it's important to appear to be in demand by important people. Color the message slips pink, fill in your name, and scatter them around your desk.

While You Were Out	While You Were Out
Important Message for _____	Important Message for _____
date _____ time _____	date _____ time _____
SENATOR BRADLEY OF NEW JERSEY — NEEDS TO SPEAK TO YOU URGENTLY ABOUT CONFIDENTIAL, HIGH-LEVEL MATTER.	PRESIDENT OF GENERAL MOTORS — WANTS TO RETAIN YOU TO HANDLE MAJOR ACQUISITION OF THE NATION OF JAPAN BY G.M. PLEASE CALL ASAP!
While You Were Out	**While You Were Out**
Important Message for _____	Important Message for _____
date _____ time _____	date _____ time _____
ARNOLD SCHWARZENEGGER WOULD LIKE TO MEET YOU AT THE HEALTH CLUB TO LIFT WEIGHTS WITH YOU.	JUDGE HIRAM GOODFELLOW WOULD LIKE TO DISCUSS DECISION HE'S ABOUT TO MAKE IN CASE INVOLVING YOUR CLIENT TO MAKE SURE THAT IT IS SATISFACTORY TO YOU!

STEALING COMPETITORS' CLIENTS

Sure, you can just go out and try to convince prospects that you can outperform their current counsel. But your chances of success are a whole lot better if you get some of your competitor's letterhead and send one of the following letters to their clients.

Dear _____:

    If you don't pay our bill within the next twenty-four hours, we shall be forced to cease representing you and to commence collection action. Please make your payment by certified check or bank check.

                     Sincerely yours,

Dear _____:

    You have probably heard rumors to the effect that the principal partners in our corporate, litigation, tax, and environmental areas have bolted to other law firms. We are writing to assure you that this is not true or, in the alternative, if it is true, it will have no significant impact on our continuing to do business.

    We trust that you will remain loyal to us in these trying times.

                     Sincerely,

P.S. If you hear of any firms looking for somebody in my area of practice, I would appreciate it if you would pass my name and phone number along to them.

Dear _____:

    This is to inform you that, effective immediately, we will be raising all of our lawyers' hourly billing rates by fifty percent. This fee increase has become necessary in order for us to continue to live in the style to which we have become accustomed. We are confident that you will understand, and thank you in advance for your acquiescence. These increases will be retroactive to January 1, 1992.

                     Very truly yours,

Dear _____:

    We have decided to take on representation of your competitor, _____ Corporation. While we recognize that this may appear to present a conflict of interest, the amount of legal fees that we expect to receive from them is so staggering that we don't care.

    We do not want you to feel that we are dumping you. Quite the contrary. Though my time and the time of the three other partners and two senior associates who have been working on your matters will be consumed by our new client, we have several inexperienced associates who are willing to cut their teeth on your work.

    We appreciate your continuing patronage.

                     Yours most truly,

YOU'RE SWELL. IN FACT, YOU'RE SUPREME!

Join Sandra, Clarence, et al., on the highest court in the land.
Just paste your picture in the spot marked *X* and you're on.
No appointment necessary! And no fear of being Borked!

ABOUT THE AUTHORS

Arnie Kanter is a management consultant to law firms and investment banks, the author of four satirical books on law firm mismanagement, and (*gasp*) a lawyer.

Jodi Kanter is a writer and actress living in Chapel Hill, North Carolina, and is the daughter of a (*gasp*) lawyer.

Tony Tallarico is the author and illustrator of more than 1,000 children's books. He has nothing to do with lawyers.